A Roadmap
To Career Success

25 Tips For College Bound Students

Second Edition
By John G. Bendt

A Roadmap to Career Success – 25 Tips For College Bound Students may be purchased for educational use. For information please write to: Education Markets Department, Career Mentor Press, LLC,1120 Tonkawa Rd, Long Lake, MN 55356.

*Visit our website at **www.careerprepteens.com***

ISBN 978-0-9790707-1-6

"*A Roadmap To Career Success* is packed with information for anyone preparing for a successful work life. From early exploration of potential careers through skill building to job attainment, the 25 tips provided in this text are sure to create a successful scenario for high school and college students looking toward their working futures. I wish all early high school students could have this information in a format like this that is easy to read, understand, and implement. This text will bring clarity, decrease anxiety, and generally provide insight necessary to career success. This is definitely a book I will recommend to students and clients. I've already passed it on to my high school freshman daughter!"
Elisabeth Bennett, Ph.D. Associated Professor, Gonzaga University Licensed Psychologist, Washington State

"As someone whose career has depended on the quality of our people, I applaud John Bendt's *Roadmap to Career Success*. He's written a simple, easy-to-read eye-opener for young students who want to understand a world that often seems way too far over the horizon. John's insights from his years in the business world and deep passion for helping young people come through loud and clear."
Steve Wehrenberg, Executive Vice President, Director of Strategic Planning, Campbell Mithun, Minneapolis, MN.

"Mr. Bendt has provided a great resource full of helpful tips for students. Chapter 2 with information on hard and soft skills is a 'must read' for anyone entering the world of work!"
Deb Crapes, Career Specialist, Spokane, WA.

"John Bendt's, *A Roadmap To Career Success,* is a goldmine of career achievement tips, techniques and tools all young people should know, but *few* do. Consistently applied, this book will help young people find the right career, and establish competitive advantage in the job marketplace. Bendt's forty years of solid business experience serve to make the book practical, realistic and credible. It reads like a personal conversation with a mentor. Buy a copy for your ninth grader – I'm buying copies for my grandkids and any other kids with whom I come in contact."
Roger E. Wenschlag, Self-Employed Human Resource Development Consultant & Trainer – former teacher, vocational school director, naval officer, father of two and grandfather. Minneapolis, MN

"Technology is affecting all of us on a daily basis. The rate of change is on an exponential scale, and we must all adapt to be successful. Career planning has never been more important for youth today. Emphasis should be given to building basic hard and soft skills that will allow you to adapt to changing conditions. *A Roadmap To Career Success* is a straight forward approach to identifying your strengths and understanding how to acquire and improve skills for a career in a field that is interesting, challenging & rewarding to you. If you love what you do, it's not work. Taking a few minutes to read the 25 tips will put your career on the road to your desired destination. Enjoy the ride."

Daniel O. Adams, Mechanical Engineer & Consultant to Medical Device Companies, Minneapolis, MN. – Inventor on. 45 U.S Medical Device Patents. Former Vice President of Research & Development, Boston Scientific, Vice President Research & Development, ev3, Inc.

"As Physical Therapists, we have the advantage of entering the job market with a board exam and a good college degree. Our hard skills are strong. It is the soft skills that set one therapist apart from another. Communication and teamwork will make or break one's effectiveness in working with patients and other health professionals. This book provides students with an excellent understanding of the importance of soft skills, and teaches them there is more to a career than the textbooks."

Lois Neaton, Physical Therapist, Manager, Minneapolis, MN.

Today competition for the best jobs is tremendously fierce and competitive. John Bendt has presented a roadmap of 25 steps to help guide the reader through career discovery, selection, preparation and networking to achieve success in their career choice. He presents a practical set of steps that will guide the reader in building the skills necessary to create opportunities for themselves in the competitive workplace. This book is an excellent choice for high school or college students who are interested in moving to the front of the line to accomplish a successful career choice. I strongly recommend this book to all who seek to create the best opportunities in their career selection!

Thomas Brinsko, President / CEO, YMCA of Greater Saint Paul

This book is dedicated to my mother and father who made countless sacrifices to provide opportunities for their seven children, and who taught me success is achieved with skill and hard work.

<u>ACKNOWLEDGEMENTS</u>

The concepts discussed in this book are based on a life time of lessons learned from formal education, seminars, professional literature, mentors, supervisors, co-workers, clients, friends, and over forty years of work experience in the business world. Although not all of these concepts are my original creation, it is my hope that the unique manner in which they are presented will provide students new and valuable insights, so they can better prepare for a work life that is fulfilling and successful.

I would like to express my appreciation to those who helped and encouraged me to write this book. A special thanks to Mary Brown whose encouragement and advice was invaluable. Special thanks also to Brian Blankenburg for his insights, and to my wife, children and their spouses for their encouragement and critique of the various drafts of this book.

Thanks also to the following people who helped me make this book better: Robert Bendt, Kristen Bendt, Tom Brown, Matt Brown, Steve Chase, Mary Cranston, Allison Cranston, Courtney Cranston, Dave Harris, Ron Harvieux, Jim Hughes, Tom Kingston, Mary Kingston, Elmer Lemon, Betty Lemon, Susan Moseley, Steve Moseley, Michael Ricci Jr., Buck Roach, Eric Roach, Ginny Randolph, Carol Roland, Gary Ringus, Barb Schmidt, Bob Schmidt, Donna Schuler, Shawn Stender, Donna Villand, Steve Villand, Gary Williams.

C O N T E N T S

Preface

A Message To College Bound Students:

Imagine you're at your five year high school class reunion. You graduated from college in four years, and have completed the first year in a job that was not your first choice. The job is not very exciting. To make matters worse, you're listening to Kristen and her friends Abby and Katie raving about Dennis Ryan's new sports car. Worse yet, Dennis got the job you really wanted. So you're very irritated when Kristen adds, "Man, he's got it made! Great job! He loves what he does and makes good money."

Sarcastically you say, "Yeah, he had the inside track. He knew the president of LaFrieda Foods and lots of other people there. He's probably a nephew or something!"

Kristen responds, "No way, I heard he started exploring occupations in high school and discovered he liked marketing. Hey, he took Spanish, and guess who LaFrieda's major customers are – yes, Latinos. He belonged to the sales and marketing club in high school and competed in the club's state and national competitions. Then he minored in Spanish in college and worked part time in a Spanish-oriented grocery store near his campus. He even worked a summer internship with – guess who – LaFrieda's advertising agency, and because of his Spanish skills and work at the grocery store, he was assigned to work on the LaFrieda account."

"Wow!" Abby says, "Sounds to me like anyone who interviewed against him didn't have a chance! He had

the whole plan in place when most of us weren't even thinking of what we were going to do after college."

What do you think? Was Dennis Ryan just lucky, or was he traveling along a well-thought-out career plan? How about you? Have you thought seriously about what you want to do for a living, and what it will take to get a great job after college? A job you'll really love – one that will make it possible for you to have things like a great car, apartment, or the latest electronics.

Do you want to have a career full of work you love to do? Or do you want to end up like many college graduates who have no clear direction, or take jobs that are not what they really had hoped to do? Do you want to get stuck in work that is boring? Do you want to experience false starts in pursuing majors and end up with more college debt, because it takes more time to graduate?

If you do it right, you can avoid these mistakes. You can find work that is satisfying and fulfilling, and earn an income that can enable you to pursue the lifestyle you desire.

You may be thinking; "Are you crazy? Who the heck thinks about that stuff at my age? I'll figure it out later." I would like to challenge you to start thinking about your future now. Start an exploration to find work you would really love to do, and start preparing yourself to make that happen. Many of your peers won't have the ambition to take up this challenge. Will you? If you do, you can dramatically improve the quality of your future life.

I'd like to help you be proactive in preparing yourself to achieve happiness and success in your work life.

I've worked in sales, marketing, and management consulting jobs for over forty years. When my four children were entering high school, I taught them how to find an occupation they could get excited about and how to prepare themselves to win the job they wanted. All are happy and doing well in their careers today.

This book will help you learn how to do your career planning right. I know of no other book, written for students, that describes the big picture of how to achieve happiness and success in one's work life. That's why I decided to write this book.

Understanding the big picture enables you to see how things interrelate. It's like having an "inside tip" to know how things work. This can help you prepare for the future, because you will be able to make wise choices in the _present_ that will improve your ability to succeed and gain what you want in the _future_.

Throughout this book, you'll see how choices you make at varying stages of your school years and work life can affect the achievement of your personal and career goals.

Jump in and read it. Use the book as a reference as you progress through high school and college and into your work life. If you use the tools described, you will likely achieve happiness and success!

Confucius, the philosopher of ancient China, said many wise things, and here is one thought you should take to heart as you read on: **"If you enjoy what you do, you'll never work another day in your life"**

Introduction

Competition – A Fact of Life

When I was in high school, my idea of competition was pretty much limited to sports, or attracting the girl I wanted to date. A few of my friends were exceptional students, so they had a broader view that included earning a scholarship to college. None of us, however, had a clue about the role competition would play later on in our work lives.

Being clueless certainly isn't an advantage, because **your ability to compete is the single most important factor in determining the success you will have in your work life.**

This is true for all occupations! It's a fact of life you can't avoid. Eventually you'll have to compete for a job. Think about it. For every job you want, there will be many others who will also want it. To get the job, you'll have to prove you are the best choice! Employers consider multiple applicants for jobs, no matter what the job is, and competition is greatest for the best jobs. Today's global economy makes the competition even tougher, because you'll be competing with workers in the rest of the world.

You'll come out on top if you know how to create *skill advantages*. For example, the football running back that is faster, shiftier and stronger than other contenders gets the starting position. Scholarships are won by students with the best academic records, resumes, and potential for success. It is the same in the workplace. To win in the workplace, you must **differentiate yourself from others by creating skill advantages an**

employer will value. Understanding and creating these advantages is essential, if you want to be able to compete effectively throughout your work life.

This book will teach you how to create skill advantages. I've called it a roadmap, because it will guide you through a journey to develop a rewarding and successful career. The journey starts while you are in high school, and continues through college and into your work life. To make a successful journey, **you must make choices in the present, which will greatly improve your ability to succeed and gain what you want in the future.**

If you use the tools described in each step of the journey, you can create significant skill advantages by the time you apply for the first job in your occupation and throughout your career. You will be miles ahead on the road to success.

The career roadmap described in this book will take you through the following steps:

- Exploring occupations.
- Identifying skills employers value.
- Bundling your skills to create advantage.
- Selecting your occupation / industry.
- Developing your skills.
- Learning how to market yourself.
- Learning how to find and assess job opportunities

Welcome to the journey!

Chapter 1

<u>Explore Occupations</u>

The first step in the journey is to explore occupations. Everyone faces the same question: What type of work do I want to do to earn a living? Most students your age have no idea what they want to do. That's okay. Most also haven't thought seriously about how to decide. That's not okay. Don't be one of those people who thinks that somehow, someday it will just become clear. Waiting for a job vision to just pop into your head doesn't make a lot of sense, does it? A better way is to use a simple research process to identify and explore occupations. This chapter describes the process.

Tip #1 – The best time for you to start exploring occupations is when you enter high school.

You may be saying to yourself; "Why should I do it now, when I have plenty of time, and there are so many other ways I can spend my time?" Here are some good reasons:

- **It takes time to explore occupations and find one you will be excited about.** Thousands of jobs are available. If you don't know what the jobs are, and the nature of the work, you rob yourself of finding work you'll enjoy and find fulfilling. A great share of your life will be your work life. Do you want to spend it being bored or unhappy?

- **It's much easier to get help** researching occupations because school resources are available, and people working in the occupations are very willing to help you learn about their work.

- **You'll have the opportunity to gain a mentor early in your life.** A mentor is an experienced person who wants to help you. He or she can provide valuable advice regarding career opportunities and the skills required to take advantage of them.

- **Your exploration of occupations will provide great opportunities to learn and practice some important skills that will make you more competitive in the workplace.** These skills will give you a huge head start over peers who choose to do other things with their time

- **You can choose your high school classes and extra curricular activities to support your possible career choices.**

- **You could save thousands of dollars in tuition costs and get an earlier start earning an income,** because you'll be able to complete your college degree in the shortest period of time by taking the courses that support your career focus.

As you can see, if you start your exploration of occupations when you enter high school, you'll benefit greatly in the future. Use the following steps to guide your exploration.

Identify Occupational Alternatives

The task of identifying occupations that interest you can be daunting, especially when you have limited knowledge of occupation alternatives and what they entail. So where do you start? Fortunately, the first step, building a broad list of occupational alternatives, has already been completed for you by the U.S. Department of Labor.

This department publishes the *Occupational Outlook Handbook*, a source of career information. Revised every two years, the *Handbook* describes what workers do on the job, working conditions, the training and education needed, earnings, and expected job prospects in a wide range of occupations. Occupations are listed in categories so that it is easier to screen and zero in on ones that interest you.

A companion reference source is the *Career Guide to Industries.* It provides information on careers by industry, including the nature of the industry, working conditions, occupations in the industry, training, advancement, earnings, benefits, and employment outlook. Both are available on the internet at www.bls.gov.

In addition to these Department of Labor resources, talk to your high school counselor about using career information software along with interest and aptitude tests your school may have available to help you determine your interest in potential careers.

Another excellent way to expand your exploration is to talk to your parents and relatives about their jobs to learn about their occupation and the reasons they chose it.

How Do I Select?

By the time you have reached high school, you have a fairly good idea of your academic interests and strengths, as well as your personality traits and personal likes and dislikes. If you are unsure, however, talk to your counselor at your high school about the testing tools that are available to help you identify your interests, personality traits, and aptitude for various occupations.

Rely on your self knowledge to build a list of occupations you would like to explore. Ask yourself the three questions stated below to screen and select occupations for your list.

- Which occupations do I find interesting?
- Could I be good at this occupation with education and training?
- Will this occupation meet my lifestyle needs?

Examples of lifestyle needs are things like the standard of living you desire, where you want to live, being married or single, having children, the amount of hours or travel you are willing to devote to your work, etc.

Be curious, don't limit your selections. Explore a wide variety of occupations that meet these criteria. You'll have time to narrow your list as you learn more about each occupation. A broad search, will give you more confidence when you make a final selection.

Also if you have selected occupations that occur in multiple industries, you'll need to screen industry alternatives. For example, if you decided to select an occupation such as sales, marketing, accounting, finance, engineering, or manufacturing production, you will eventually need to pick an industry in which to work. Use the *Career Guide To Industries to* screen industry alternatives and build a list of the ones that you find interesting and would like to explore.

Bring The Occupations To Life

There is no better way to fully understand what it is like to work in an occupation than to talk to someone who is actually doing it. Accomplishing this may seem more challenging and intimidating than it really is. Besides, completing this step will give you practical experience in using skills you will need to effectively compete when you enter the workplace. These skills include networking to find people to talk to, soliciting their cooperation to meet with you, and conducting the meeting.

"But I don't feel comfortable doing that!" That was the reaction of my children when I described this process to them when they attended high school.

"Why do you feel uncomfortable", I asked?

"Because I'm not sure I know how to do it, and I'll be totally embarrassed and awkward talking with someone I don't really know," they answered.

I responded, *"I'll coach you through the steps. If you make a mistake or are awkward during the meeting, what are the consequences aside from some embarrassment? Would you rather postpone learning how to do these things to when you're actually competing for a job you want, and the consequence of mistakes in an interview could disqualify you? Plus the people you meet will know you are a student, and they will be helpful and understanding."*

This dialog reinforces the next important tip.

Tip #2 – **Learning to compete in the workplace requires practice just as learning any new skill requires practice.**

In sports you would not think of just showing up for games without ever practicing. And usually we learn to play a sport at a young age when we are awkward and make mistakes. With practice we become more skilled and proficient. The same is true for acquiring skills to network and conduct a meeting.

Build Your Contact List

For the purpose of illustration, let's say you're interested in exploring a career in sales. Sales representatives work in a variety of industries. How do you find someone in this occupation that would be willing to discuss his or her job with you? And how do you find someone in the industries you have targeted to explore?

Start by asking your parents if they know any sales representatives in the industries you selected. If they don't, expand your search in the following ways:

- Request that your parents ask their friends and co- workers for referrals.

- Ask your friends if they know anyone in sales. Ask their parents if they can help you, or if they would ask their friends and co-workers for referrals.

- Ask your teachers for a referral. Request that they ask their friends and co-workers for referrals.

- Go to your school career center and ask them for help with a referral.

As you can see, the web of contacts grows larger and larger as you progress with your search. This is called networking, and eventually you'll identify someone in the target occupation who has some connection to people you know. It's always more comfortable to contact someone you don't know when you can mention the person's name who helped you with the referral.

Schedule A Meeting

An easy approach to scheduling a meeting is to ask the person who gave you the referral to find out if the person is willing to meet with you. After you receive confirmation that the person is available, simply call him or her to schedule a time and place to meet at their convenience.

The people you wish to talk to will be impressed by the maturity you are demonstrating. They will be eager to help you learn about their occupation and will be flattered you called. In fact, If they have children, they'll probably be thinking, "This would be a great thing for my children to do." Given this, don't let fear stop you from requesting meetings.

Prepare For The Meeting

You'll need to be organized so you can make the most of this opportunity and respect the time of the person you are meeting. This is your chance to deepen your understanding of the occupation by learning about the experiences of someone actually doing the work.

Conducting a successful meeting requires skill. A key meeting tool is an agenda. An agenda keeps a meeting focused and ensures relevant topics are addressed.

Using an agenda for your meeting provides an opportunity for you to gain experience with this tool, and to demonstrate that you're well organized and serious about your meeting. Email the agenda to the person prior to your meeting so that he or she will know what information you are seeking. A sample agenda is shown below.

AGENDA
Discussion With Keri Lee, Physical Therapist

1) Describe your current knowledge of the work of a physical therapist. Ask Ms Lee if your understanding is accurate

2) Would you please discuss the work you perform as a physical therapist?

3) What does a typical day in your job entail?

4) What do you like best and least about your job?

5) What key skills do you need to do your job?

6) What type of education and work experiences are needed to get a job?

7) How did you know you wanted a career in physical therapy? What related careers did you explore, or should I consider exploring?

8) What is a starting salary and are there good advancement opportunities?

9) Are there job openings now and will there be growth over next 5 years?

10) What advice can you offer for pursuing a career in physical therapy?

11) May I call you in the future if I have more questions or to seek your advice?

Figure 1.0

The agenda on the previous page lists key questions you can ask to gather information about any occupation. Its use will keep the meeting flowing. To illustrate, let's assume you're interested in exploring the occupation of physical therapy. .

Conduct The Meeting

It's important that you be well groomed and dressed appropriately for your meeting. Yes, you guessed it, jeans and T-Shirts, or the latest clothing fad are too casual.

Tip #3 – A good appearance is important, because people form opinions of you based on appearance and first impressions.

You experience this in school. Your classmates form opinions of others based on how they dress and the way they look. It is no different in the professional work world.

It's also important to greet the person you are meeting with a smile, eye contact, and a firm hand shake. Such a greeting communicates warmth, confidence, and an eagerness to know the person. If you're shy, it's very important that you force yourself to overcome your shyness when greeting people. Shyness can be very difficult to overcome, but it truly is a matter of determination and practice. A good way to practice is in front of a mirror or with your parents. This technique provides you the opportunity to see yourself in action and get feedback from others.

Start your meeting by thanking the person for meeting with you. Take some time to build rapport by talking about comfortable things like where you go to school, grade level, where you live, and why you have an interest in physical therapy. Make sure to be yourself and show your personality. This is a great opportunity to begin an ongoing relationship with an experienced professional. After this introductory conversation, refer to your agenda and move through the agenda items.

To address the first item, summarize your current understanding of the occupation. It's best to do this with written notes which you can refer to during your meeting. Telling the person what you know about the occupation will help her or him confirm the accuracy of your understanding and correct it where necessary. It also demonstrates you're serious.

I've had experiences meeting with students who claimed they were interested in exploring a career in sales and marketing, but did no research ahead of time. They obviously didn't make a good first impression, but more importantly, they failed to take full advantage of the meeting opportunity, because they were unable to ask questions which would have increased their understanding.

Tip #4 – Being prepared to make the most of a meeting is an important skill you will need in the workplace.

No matter what type of work you do, you will attend or lead meetings. *A skillful meeting leader makes meetings more effective and gets noticed by those who make decisions regarding job promotions.* Practicing this skill in these types of meetings gives you valuable experience which will help you to develop this very important skill.

Agenda items two through ten are designed to give you real world information about the occupation and make it come alive. Discussions around these points will provide opportunities for clarifying questions so that you can develop a much deeper understanding of what it is like to work in the occupation.

End your meeting by expressing your appreciation for the help you've received. Also ask the person if it would be okay for you to call him or her in the future with more questions or a request for advice. This request can open the opportunity for you to gain a mentor, which is a valuable resource. Think of a mentor as a coach who wants to help you succeed. Also explore the possibility of job shadowing with this person. Job shadowing means that you would spend some time with the person on the job to experience what it is like.

Tip #5 – A mentor relationship is extremely valuable. The mentor will share her or his experience and advice, thus giving you a tremendous advantage in developing your career.

Summarize Your Meeting

Take notes during your meeting to record important information. Taking notes will assist you to write a report of your meeting later. It also tells the person that you value what he or she is saying.

Write a report summarizing the information you've gathered as soon after the meeting as possible. See Figure 1.1 on the next page for a suggested format. Just fill in the details under each heading, and you will have an excellent record of your meeting. Keep the report on file, because it will be very useful later in a number of ways.

**Career Discussion With
Ms. Keri Lee, Physical Therapist
September 8, 2006**

Occupation: Physical Therapist

Description of Work Performed

Job Likes & Dislikes

Key Skills Required

Education / Work Experience Required

Occupation Outlook in Five Years

Salary / Advancement Opportunities

Advice Received

Figure 1.1

Follow-up

Immediately after your meeting, you should send a hand written thank you note to the person you met. It's very important to express your appreciation, and the person you talked with will appreciate your note. This is also a good way to start building an ongoing relationship with a professional. It is never too early to start building a network of people from whom you can learn

Chapter 2

<u>Skills Employers Value</u>

The second step in your journey to career success is to understand the skills employers value. Just as every competitive sport has key skills that are important to winning the game, success in the workplace also requires key skills.

Tip #6 – The more highly you develop skills that are important to employers, the more successful you will become.

These include hard skills and soft skills. It is important that you understand their nature and how they complement each other.

Hard Skills

Every occupation and industry requires a unique set of skills. For example, engineers need to know the science and math required for engineering projects. A sales representative needs to develop selling expertise and an understanding of the customer's needs in his or her industry. Doctors need to know how to diagnose and treat the diseases they encounter in their specialty.

Skills required to perform the work of a given occupation in a given industry are called hard skills. Hard skills are learned in college while pursuing a specific degree. They can also be learned in training programs or while working on the job.

The U.S. Department of Labor's *Occupational Outlook Handbook* is a great source for identifying hard skill requirements for the occupations you are exploring. Also discussing hard skill requirements with the people you meet while exploring occupations will help you more fully understand the nature of these essential skills.

Soft Skills

Soft skills, on the other hand, are required in *every occupation and industry*. Examples are the ability to work well with others and to communicate effectively. ***Think of soft skills as the skills that facilitate the effective use of hard skills.*** For example, if you are working on a group project, the group will be more effective if there is good communication and teamwork. Employers value employees who have good soft skills, because they know these employees will make their company or organization more successful.

Many types of soft skills are required in the workplace. They can be categorized in the following way:

- *Ability to Work Well With Others*
  Working well with others requires the ability to relate with co-workers and being a good teammate. It's also essential to be a good listener and to communicate effectively with others verbally and in writing.

- *Problem Solving*
  Solving problems requires the ability to find and use information to determine the cause of a problem. Critical thinking and creativity to conceive alternative solutions, are also key skills used by effective problem solvers.

- *Organizational Skills*
  Important organizational skills needed in all occupations include the ability to set priorities, organize and manage work activities, and make efficient use of time.

- *Computer Skills*
  Proficiency in the use of the internet, plus word-processing, spreadsheet, data base, and presentation software, is essential in jobs today.

- *Management Skills*
  The ability to plan, organize, and control are key management skills for all organizations whether they are businesses, healthcare facilities, schools, social service agencies, government, etc.

  Planning enables a manager to set objectives, strategies, and tactics, to accomplish goals. Organizing provides the structure and resources to implement the plans. Monitoring and measuring the implementation of the plan provides control, so that changes can be made if goals are not being achieved.

  Effective managers also know how to use information and judgment to make good decisions. They have good leadership and coaching skills. They are good listeners, and know how to motivate and persuade others. They are able to resolve conflicts that may arise between people and know how to promote teamwork.

- *Personal Attributes*
  Character qualities such as being honest, trustworthy, loyal, responsible, dependable, empathetic, and courteous are highly valued by employers. When coupled with a strong work ethic, self motivation, curiosity, self confidence, flexibility, adaptability, and the ability to work under pressure, it makes an employee very effective, and one that co-workers like to work with.

With the exception of the skills I've labeled personal attributes, all of the soft skills listed above can be learned in schools or training programs. It is important to recognize, however, they only have value when put into practice. Personal attributes, on the other hand, are derived from your will and self-discipline. For example, you decide how hard you will work, and whether you will be honest and trustworthy. Your self-discipline drives how self motivated, responsible and dependable you will be.

Figure 2.0 on the following pages lists the soft skills discussed above in a summary format that may be more convenient for your future reference.

SUMMARY OF IMPORTANT SOFT SKILLS

Skills for Working Well With Others
- Good verbal and written communication.
- Interpersonal skills – communicating / relating with co-workers.
- Being a good listener – improves communication and teamwork.
- Teamwork – accomplishing tasks by working with others.
- Ability to conduct effective meetings.
- Understanding and relating to people of different gender, races or cultures.

Problem Solving Skills
- Critical thinking – questioning, challenging, proposing alternatives.
- Research skills – finding information to determine causes of problems.
- Quantitative skills – use of numerical data to study or resolve questions.
- Creativity – ability to conceive new ideas or solutions to problems.

Organizational Skills
- Being organized in your work.
- Time management – make efficient use of your time by planning.
- Ability to prioritize and manage things on the job and in your personal life.

Computer Skills
- Ability to use word-processing, spreadsheet, data base, and presentation software.
- Ability to use the internet.

Management Skills

- Ability to plan – set objectives, strategies, and tactics to accomplish goals.
- Ability to organize – provide and structure resources to implement plans.
- Ability to control – monitor implementation of plans / measure achievement of goals and make necessary changes if goals are not being met.
- Decision making skills – use information and judgment to make good decisions.
- Leadership – lead and support others to accomplish goals.
- Coaching / Training – show others how to do something.
- Persuasion – get others to consider or accept a different point of view.
- Conflict management – resolve conflicts between people you work with.

Personal Attributes

- Being honest and trustworthy.
- Responsible and dependable.
- Empathetic and courteous.
- Strong work ethic.
- Goal / objective directed.
- Self motivated – show initiative, drive to accomplish, improve skills.
- Curiosity – desire to know more about the present & next steps.
- Self confidence – able to handle own work, ask questions when necessary, correct mistakes, accept constructive criticism positively with a desire to improve.
- Ability to work under pressure to meet deadlines or overcome constraints.
- Demonstrate flexibility and adaptability when faced with changing conditions.

Figure 2.0

Chapter 3

<u>Bundle Skills To Create Advantage</u>

The previous chapter identified skills that are important to employers. The next step in your journey is to learn how to bundle them to create a competitive advantage. The goal is to create a combination of hard and soft skills that will distinguish you from others.

The hard skills required in any occupation are a given, and you won't succeed if you're incompetent in these skills. You can create a significant competitive advantage if you excel at your occupation's hard skills, but if you also possess excellent soft skills, your advantage will be much greater.

Tip #7 – Highly developed soft skills play a big role in creating competitive advantage.

Over the course of my business career, I've had the unpleasant task of firing people. In most cases these people were competent in their hard skills, but their serious soft skill weaknesses prevented them from performing their job in a satisfactory manner.

That's why it's extremely important for you to develop and excel at the soft skills that are most important to your occupation. For example, if you are a sales representative, soft skills such as verbal and written communication, interpersonal skills, and teamwork are very important. You'll also need to be well organized, use time efficiently, prioritize your activities, and be able to use word processing and presentation software.

If you're a computer systems analyst, you'll need strong problem solving skills, analytical skills, and the ability to think logically to solve computer problems and apply computer technology to meet your organization's needs. You'll also require good communication and interpersonal skills, plus the ability to work effectively on a team.

If you are a lawyer, you'll need good writing and verbal skills. You must be able to research, analyze, and think logically to handle complex cases and unique legal problems. You will also need to be able to work well with people to win the respect and confidence of clients and associates.

If you're a physical therapist, strong interpersonal skills are required to be able to educate patients about their treatments. Good writing and verbal skills are needed to communicate with other healthcare providers and document therapy treatments.

A word of caution however, just because the importance of some soft skills vary by occupation, it doesn't mean you can be incompetent in the ones of lesser importance. Your goal should be to create an advantage by achieving excellence in the highest priority ones for your occupation, but be competent in all of them.

Always remember the combination of strong hard and soft skills will make you a winner because you will offer tremendous value to your employer!

Learn Which Soft Skills Have The Greatest Importance

The U.S. Department of Labor's *Occupational Outlook Handbook* lists soft skill requirements for all the occupations described. For example, the following direct quote describes the soft skill requirements for financial management positions.

> "Candidates for financial management positions need a broad range of skills. Interpersonal skills are important because these jobs involve managing people and working as part of a team to solve problems. Financial managers must have excellent communication skills to explain complex financial data. Because financial managers work extensively with various departments in their firm, a broad overview of the business is essential. Financial managers should be creative thinkers and problem-solvers, applying their analytical skills to business. They must be comfortable with the latest computer technology. As financial operations increasingly are affected by the global economy, financial managers must have knowledge of international finance. Proficiency in a foreign language also may be important."

The people you met when researching occupations are also great sources for identifying high priority soft skills for the occupations you're considering. The agenda shown in the first chapter under the heading, *Prepare For The Meeting,* included a discussion of key skills required for the occupation. Use the information collected in your meeting, and don't hesitate to call these people again to clarify or improve your understanding of skill requirements.

Write down the key soft skills for each occupation you have explored. A suggested format to use for this record is illustrated in Figure 3.0. File the form so you can refer to it in the future. It will be very useful later when you create a plan to develop your soft skills.

> Sales Representative
>
> **Key Soft Skills**
>
> 1) Verbal / Written Communication
> 2) Interpersonal Skills
> 3) Teamwork
> 4) Being Organized
> 5) Time Management
> 6) Ability to Prioritize
> 7) Software: Word Processing
>   Presentation Software
>
> **Figure 3.0**

Soft-Skills-of-Universal-Importance

Let's play a "what if game". If you were the owner of a business or the coach of a sport, I'm confident you would want all your employees or team members to be hard working, highly motivated, responsible, dependable, goal directed, self-confident, able to perform under pressure, and capable of adapting to changing conditions. I'm also sure, however, you've experienced working with people in jobs or school projects where you've noticed varying levels of effort and dependability. If you've participated in organized sports, you most likely have seen teammates with varying levels of motivation and confidence. The employees and teammates described in the first sentence are an ideal – not always reality. However, it's a fact that employers and coaches desire the ideal.

Tip #8 – **The fact that employers desire the ideal in an employee, creates a great opportunity for those willing to practice the personal attributes described above. By combining these attributes and other soft skills with hard skill excellence, you'll be highly valuable to employers and experience great success.**

If you remember only one tip from this book, remember this one! Bundling skills in this manner is the perfect way to distinguish yourself from others. It's the cornerstone upon which you should build your career. It's the key to career success!

Chapter 4

Select An Occupation & Industry

According to the roadmap, you're now crossing the midpoint of your journey to career success. At this point, you've just graduated from high school and are about to start college. It's time to make an <u>initial selection</u> of the occupation and industry you want to pursue. Obviously this is a big and important crossroad. All of the remaining steps in the journey are shaped by the choice you make, since each occupation has its own set of skill requirements.

Tip #9 – To build skill advantages, you need to know where you want to go with your career.

This is true because skill advantages vary by occupation. Advantages for a sales representative will be different from a lawyer, computer systems analyst, doctor, nurse, physical therapist, marketing manager, engineer, accountant, teacher, scientist, etc.

During your high school years you've researched a number of occupations and industries, and at this stage you should have narrowed the number of alternatives. Now it's time to pick one. Obviously you can change your mind later if you discover you would rather be on a different path. However, if you did a good job of researching your alternatives, you should have confidence in proceeding.

Let's talk about several tools you can use to help make your selection. One tool is to rate your alternatives on a set of criteria. The factors you originally used to screen occupations are good rating criteria.

For each occupation on your list, assign a rating from 1 to 5 (with 5 being the best) for each criteria. Total the scores and rank the alternatives from highest to lowest. Look at the worksheet below. It illustrates this technique for four occupations.

OCCUPATION	INTERESTING	I CAN EXCEL	LIFESTYLE GOALS	TOTAL
Journalist	5	5	5	15
Advertising Account Executive	4	4	4	12
Marketing Manager	4	4	4	12
Public Relations Specialist	3	4	3	10

Figure 4.0

The screening criteria Include your level of interest in the occupation, assessment of your ability to excel in the occupation, and whether your lifestyle needs and goals can be met.

As you can see, these criteria are listed across the top of the worksheet, along with a column for a total ranking score. The occupation alternatives are listed in the first column. When assigning your rating, it's useful to consider the occupations in relation to each other. For example, when rating "journalist" for level of interest, consider how interesting you find it relative to the other alternatives. The total of the ratings will allow you to rank the occupations from highest to lowest per your key screening criteria. This technique helps to clarify your thinking and highlight differences.

Another technique you can use is to analyze pros and cons. With this technique prepare a list of the pros and cons for each occupation. To help you build this list, refer to the reports you wrote to summarize the information you collected in meetings with practitioners of the occupations. Next compare the results from one alternative to another to identify differences to help you make a selection. It's important to keep in mind, however, every occupation has some elements that are mundane or unexciting. The key measure is to judge the overall satisfaction you will experience.

The following table is an example of this technique.

Pros & Cons Analysis	
PROS	**CONS**
Journalist Use my investigative and writing skills to inform the public about local, state, national, international events and current issues. Be part of a team to report the news on a daily basis. Opportunity to interpret news or offer opinions as a broadcast news analyst or columnist.	Jobs involve irregular hours, night and weekend work. Constant pressure to meet deadlines. Slower than average employment growth expected.

PROS	CONS
Advertising Account Executive	
Opportunity to work in an exciting, fast paced environment.	Long work hours including evenings and weekends.
Use my management and communication skills to co-ordinate ad agency resources to create great advertising for clients.	Short and changing project deadlines. Low starting salary.
Gain new experiences by working with a variety of clients.	Substantial travel.
High earnings potential.	
Marketing Manager	
Use my marketing skills to develop strategies and programs to market my company's products or services.	Long work hours. High pressure to meet objectives.
Satisfaction of beating competitors.	Strong competition for entry level job and job promotions.
Opportunity to supervise supporting staff.	
High earnings potential and opportunity to be a candidate for top management position.	
Public Relations Specialist	
Use writing skills and creativity to help clients build and maintain a positive relationship with the public.	Work schedules can be irregular with changing project deadlines.
Opportunity to organize special events.	Strong competition for entry level job and job promotions.
Opportunity to travel.	Potential for substantial travel.
Good earnings potential	Figure 4.1

Perhaps now, you can better understand the wisdom and importance of starting your exploration of occupations in high school. By being proactive, and following the roadmap, you've built a list of interesting alternatives. By talking to people who are working in the occupation, you gained a realistic understanding of what the work is like. You're well positioned to make an informed choice.

Compare this with your peers who chose not to plan. Most likely they have no definitive idea of the work they would like to do. They are off to college with the hope a job vision will magically pop into their head. *Tip #9 (To build skill advantages, you need to know where you want to go with your career)* surely is not working for them, and they will have a long way to go to catch up to you. You have a direction, and can now actively start to build skill advantages to succeed.

"Wait a minute", you say. "What if I cannot make a final choice yet? What if I'm still not sure?" If this happens, you need to determine what is preventing you from making a choice. You are still ahead of the game, but you need to continue to be proactive to resolve issues that are holding you back. You still have some time to make a selection. Most colleges teach basic course requirements during the first two years. Hard skill courses are usually offered during the last two years of a four year degree.

I've coached some students who continued their explorations into their first year of college before making a final choice. I've also coached a student who changed his mind about the occupation he wanted to pursue after completing some hard skill courses for his initial choice.

Importantly, in each case they continued to be proactive in evaluating their alternatives so they could make a final choice.

If you're undecided, you need to be proactive to finalize a choice too. Remember it is not realistic to expect a job vision to just pop into your head! Also you are now spending significant dollars for your education, and time is money.

Chapter 5

Develop The Required Skills

Three more steps remain on the roadmap to career success. This step addresses the development of your hard and soft skills. The next two describe effective ways to market yourself and how to find and assess job opportunities.

Previously we talked about the concept of bundling skills to create advantage. Now it is time to start developing the key skills you bundled for the occupation you selected. Since the development of occupational hard and soft skills is an ongoing effort, it is useful to think about skill development over three time frames.

- High school years
- College years
- Work years

Understanding how you can develop your skills over time, enables you to make choices in one time frame that will help you in the next. This will give you a tremendous advantage in building a successful career.

High School Years
Your high school years are the starting point for the exploration of occupations and the key skills they require. Even though you have not decided on a career direction at this point in time, many opportunities exist for you to work on key skills that will be important when

you apply for admission to college, and when you begin your work life.

Your first priority should be to refine fundamental skills such as the ability to read and write effectively, to be articulate, and apply mathematics. Without these fundamentals, it's impossible to develop competitive hard skills for any occupation. Therefore make sure your curriculum includes all the classes you need to sharpen these skills. Also if your occupational interest involves the sciences, make sure you take the science classes you need.

Lastly, some high school programs provide advanced placement classes that make it possible to earn college credit in high school. If possible, take advantage of this opportunity, so that in college, you'll have more time to take classes that focus on hard skills specific to the career you want to pursue.

Tip #10 – Participation in extra curricular activities and part-time jobs provides great opportunities to learn and practice soft skills.

Your high school years are a great time to start developing soft skills. We've already talked about how researching occupations provides the opportunity to learn and practice important skills such as networking, soliciting meetings, conducting a meeting, and finding mentors. Participation in extra curricular activities and part-time jobs are also great opportunities to learn and practice other soft skills.

For example, if you play on one of your schools athletic teams, you'll have many opportunities to demonstrate leadership, teamwork, self-motivation, self-confidence, and dependability. If you're a captain of the team, you can practice planning and organizational skills by helping to organize practices and carrying out other duties to help your coach.

You can join a school club and help lead and organize its activities. Do the same for volunteer activities. Sharpen verbal skills by joining the debate or forensics teams. Sharpen writing skills by working on the school newspaper, magazine, or year book.

Join clubs that target your occupational interests. If you're interested in business, clubs like DECA, Business Professionals of America, Future Business Leaders of America, and Junior Achievement can offer excellent experiences. The same is true for clubs targeted to other fields like healthcare (HOSA), art, music, science, computer technology, agriculture (FFA) and other technical fields (Skills USA).

Part-time jobs provide opportunities to demonstrate responsibility and dependability by always reporting to work on time and by doing a good job. You can also show initiative and self confidence by being willing to take on new duties. Interpersonal skills can be practiced in dealing with co-workers. If your job deals directly with customers, you can also practice customer service skills.

You may be thinking; "Hey, I just want to have fun in extra curricular activities, and my part-time job provides the spending money I want. Why should I make a big skill-building exercise out of it?" I'll answer your question with the following tip.

Tip #11 – The extra effort it takes to work on soft skills in extra curricular activities and part-time jobs is small, but the benefits are huge!

For example, if you're on your school's basketball team, how much extra effort does it take to practice teamwork by encouraging a struggling teammate? How much extra time does it take to offer your teammate advice?

If you've decided to participate in a volunteer activity, how much extra effort will it take to help organize or lead some part of the activity? If you want to get involved in a school club, does it take more effort to join one that supports your career interests?

When you're working a part-time job, does it take more time to demonstrate you're responsible, dependable, trustworthy and honest? Does it take more effort to work in a job that gives you a chance to use skills that are important to your career interests?

You can see my point. It doesn't take a whole lot of extra effort. It just takes some thought to look for opportunities and the will to act on them.

Use the key soft skill summaries you prepared for the occupations you are exploring to direct your attention to the skills you should target. You'll have no problem finding many opportunities to practice them without diminishing the fun of your extra curricular activities or adding extra burden to your part time job. Believe me, the skills you gain will payoff in the future!

Tip #12 – Keep a portfolio record of how you used soft skills in your activities and jobs.

The best way to record your experiences is to keep a career journal and a portfolio for all supporting documents. For example, if you were a team captain, record examples in which you demonstrated leadership and teamwork; or describe activities you planned, organized, and carried out.

If you joined a school club, explain how you planned and organized an event or activity. If you competed in competitions organized by your club, record what you did and save a copy of any awards or documents that rated your performance.

Other examples include recording the steps you took to research occupations, or explaining how you have benefited from mentors who have helped you. Save copies of articles you have written for the school newspaper or magazine. Describe work situations in which you used soft skills. For example, perhaps you resolved the complaints of an unhappy customer, or you took the initiative to offer suggestions to your supervisor to make your work more effective. If you had to plan or organize parts of your work, describe what you did. Describe how you may have used computer skills on the job.

An good way to keep a journal is to create an electronic journal using word processing software. It's easily updated and portable.

Tip #13 – Request a letter of recommendation from supervisors in all the jobs you hold.

Letters of recommendation are a powerful endorsement of your skills, especially if they reflect your performance over time in a number of jobs. Later in Chapter 6, we'll discuss how to use these letters and other skill documentation to great advantage when the time comes to compete for a job.

College Years

During this time frame, you'll have the opportunity to learn your occupation's hard skills. Your first step should be to gain admission into the right school. Apply to the ones you can afford that have the best reputation for your field of study. This is important, because your degree certifies that you've learned the hard skills for your occupation, and the prestige of your school adds value and credibility to your degree.

Colleges want to enroll top students, so the application process is very competitive. College entrance test scores, your academic record, extra curricular activities, admission essays, interviews, and personal references all play an important role in qualifying for admission.

Applying for admission to a college is in many respects like applying for a job. You have to prove you are the best qualified. The skills you've acquired in high school through occupational research, extra curricular activities, and part-time jobs will help demonstrate your qualifications. This, plus letters of recommendation from previous employers, and personal references from the professionals you know through your occupational research, will distinguish you from other applicants and provide a great advantage.

Chapter 6 discusses how to effectively market yourself. All of the principles and techniques described in that chapter can be applied to your application activities for college admission.

After you have enrolled in college, your next step is to plan your course of study so that it addresses the skill requirements of the occupation you've selected. Colleges offer assistance in planning curriculums, and it is wise to use the resource. Be sure to consult with your college advisor.

A recommendation I would make in planning your curriculum is to include psychology classes that will give you insights into how to achieve better teamwork and communication with others. Communication and teamwork are critical components to all occupations, and it is important to recognize this and develop your skills in these areas as much as possible.

You should also continue to develop your soft skills by participating in extra curricular activities or part-time jobs that provide the opportunity to practice soft skills important to the occupation you're pursuing. Continue to keep a written record in your career journal of the activities that demonstrate your use of these skills.

Tip #14 – The use of alumni mentors and internships is an absolute necessity to gain the most from your college education.

Many colleges have organized alumni networks to provide mentoring support for their students. These mentors are available to students to answer questions and enrich students' learning experience.

For example, I received a call from a marketing student who was working on a class assignment that involved the introduction of a new product. He requested help to make sure he had properly identified the pros and cons of several strategies he was considering. Our conversation helped him to clarify his thinking, but also gave him confidence that he understood the marketing principles involved. Importantly, he also established another contact with whom he could consult in the future.

Make sure you check out college resources for mentoring support. Identify the resource and how to use it. Most importantly, use it!

Many colleges provide internship opportunities for their students. Also alumni mentors and the mentors who helped you research occupations are great sources to help you identify potential internships. Internships allow you to work in your occupational field to gain real world experience. Winning an internship should be a high priority goal. To obtain an internship, you'll have to compete for it against others who have the same goal.

How do you win? You demonstrate that you're better at the skills that are important for the job, and by expressing an eagerness to learn and expand your skills. Employers hiring interns will evaluate you largely on your soft skills, attitude, and the potential you bring them. If you acted on the opportunities to develop important workplace skills while in high school and college, you'll be well prepared with examples to demonstrate your capabilities, thus greatly increasing your odds of winning the internship.

Work Years

You're now on the job with much to learn about your industry and employer. Your on the job experience will also provide opportunities to gain additional hard and soft skills. Continue to keep your career journal up to date by recording your work accomplishments and skill development. At this stage, you should address four key questions.

- What skills should I improve or acquire to excel at my current job?

- What skills should I improve or acquire to advance my career?

- How will I improve my skills or learn new ones?

- If I lost my job tomorrow, am I marketable to other companies?

Ask yourself these questions throughout your career. They are the core issues of a personal continuous improvement strategy. Following are some things you can do to continuously develop and improve your job skills:

- Express your desire to continually improve and ask your supervisor for suggestions on where you should focus.

- Seek job assignments that will "stretch" your capabilities, and help you grow.

- Read key trade or professional publications to learn about your industry and developments that could apply to your job responsibilities.

- Join trade or professional associations to keep your industry knowledge current and to meet top people in your field.

- Open a Linkedin account to grow your network and learn from posts relating to your industry.

- Use Twitter to follow people of influence in your industry.

- Attend training seminars that meet your needs for professional development.

- Use your employer's tuition reimbursement program, to take classes that will help you, or to earn a graduate degree.

- Talk to mentors that have helped you in the past.

- Recruit a career mentor who will share his or her experience to help you move your career ahead.

Tip #15 – Seeking advice from a career mentor is the most effective way to improve your skills and build your career.

All of the actions listed above are very effective methods to achieve your improvement goals. However, a career mentor is especially important. Look for someone with experience that you respect. This person can be someone in your company or industry that is willing to share her or his experience and advice to help you improve and move ahead. Such a mentoring relationship is a treasure and should be nurtured at every opportunity. Many articles have been published on how to recruit a career mentor. Find them online.

Chapter 6

Learn How To Market Yourself

Positioning

Learning how to market yourself is a critical step on the roadmap to building a successful career. A basic tool of marketing is called positioning. Companies use this tool to distinguish their products or services in ways that are important to the customers they want to attract. A product can be positioned based on such things as product attributes, quality, value, personality, and imagery. For example, I'm sure you have a very different perception of designer jean brands versus jeans sold at WalMart, or a Porsche versus a Ford.

Tip #16 – You should think of yourself as a product. Create a positioning that is based on your skill advantages.

Think about it, when you compete for a job, you're marketing yourself to the employer. You'll significantly improve your ability to win the job if you position yourself as a person with the skills the employer values. For purpose of illustration, let's assume you decided to pursue a career in marketing and are competing for an entry level marketing job with a consumer products company. You've earned a college degree with a marketing major and worked in several internships to learn required hard skills. You've identified key soft skills and personal attributes for marketing jobs and took action to learn and practice those skills through extra curricular activities, part time jobs, and internships. You're now ready to create your positioning.

Start by listing the skill advantages you bring to this job based on your accomplishments. See the example below.

LIST OF MY SKILL ADVANTAGES

Hard skills

– Business Administration B.S. degree, marketing major.

– Marketing internship with 3M – Member of team to create product promotions.

– Market research internship – Worked as interviewer of business professionals.

Soft skills

– Creativity – ability to conceive new ideas or solutions to problems.

– Good verbal and written communication skills

– Teamwork and interpersonal skills

Personal Attributes

– Self motivated and confident.

– Able to work under pressure.

– Flexible and adaptable when faced with changing conditions

Figure 6.0

Next write a concise statement that presents your skill advantages and answers the question: "Why should I hire you?" This is your positioning statement. Following is an example based on the skill advantages listed in Figure 6.0.

POSITIONING STATEMENT EXAMPLE

I've developed marketing skills by earning a BS degree (marketing major) and through work experience in two marketing internships. I've demonstrated good problem solving, teamwork, communication, and interpersonal skills. Letters of recommendation praise my self motivation, self confidence, ability to work under pressure, and flexibility when faced with changing conditions.

Figure 6.1

As you can see, this positioning statement clearly tells the employer that you offer skill advantages he or she will value.

Communicate Your Positioning

Your resume, cover letter, job interview, and personal recommendations can communicate your positioning to prospective employers. Much has been written about resume writing and how to interview for a job. It is available on the internet, and you should research this information to learn the most effective techniques. My purpose here is to highlight fundamental principles that are essential to the communication of your positioning.

Tip #17 – Understand the employer's perspective.

The employer's goal is to assess your ability to do the job. An assessment will also be made of your potential to grow and whether your personality and personal attributes are a good fit for the company. Understanding this perspective will help you provide persuasive information that will win you the job.

Tip #18 – Resumes that quickly say: "I'm qualified. I have the skills to do the job!", trigger interviews.

The primary role of your resume is to capture the employer's attention and create an opportunity for you to be interviewed. Your resume should start with an opening summary of your qualifications. Think of the opening summary as an advertisement. It must be read and be persuasive, or it won't trigger action.

An opening summary on your resume is the perfect place to use your positioning statement because it answers the question, "Why should I hire you?" To illustrate, look at the example in Figure 6.2 below.

John M. Jones
896 Young Road, Anywhere, MN 55356

612-222-4444 Home   612-222-555 Cell   jmjones@aol.com

Summary of Qualifications

- **Marketing Skills** – Earned BS Degree (marketing major) and completed two marketing internships.

- **Demonstrated** good problem solving, teamwork, communication, and interpersonal skills in past jobs.

- **Letters of Recommendation** praise my self motivation, self confidence, ability to work under pressure, and flexibility when faced with changing conditions.

Figure 6.2

This example is based on the positioning statement for the marketing job we discussed earlier in this chapter.

As you can see, it clearly and quickly communicates the skill advantages the applicant can apply to the job and differentiates him from other applicants.

I've hired new college graduates for entry level marketing positions and can assure you an opening summary such as the example above will attract the reader's attention. He or she can quickly see the applicant offers skills required to perform the job. *Many resumes are tossed because they fail to capture the employer's attention with relevant skills.*

Tip #19 – Show proof of your skills on your resume.

It is not enough to simply state you have relevant skills. You must provide evidence you can do what you claim. The best way to accomplish this is to use examples that demonstrate your skills and knowledge. Cite examples from your extra curricular and work activities. This is where your career journal pays off. It provides a ready record of the things you've done throughout your high school and college years.

Your examples should explain what you accomplished. For example, *as an intern and member of a team to create promotions, I wrote the copy for a sales brochure.* Or, *I researched competitive promotions and presented a report to management summarizing competitive offerings.* These examples demonstrate creative writing ability, analytical skill, and verbal communication capability. Your objective is to give examples in the body of your resume that prove you have the skills required to do the job.

Another way to prove your skills is through letters of recommendation. Such letters are very powerful, particularly if you can present letters spanning your high school and college years. Consistent performance makes a huge statement! I strongly recommend you request letters of recommendation from all past work supervisors so you can make such a statement.

Following is a letter of recommendation a graduating college student presented when interviewing for a position with an advertising agency. The student's name has been changed. The letter addresses part-time work she did for a market research company.

To Whom It May Concern:

My experience in working with Jacklyn Droese has been extremely positive. She is professional, well organized, flexible, and dedicated.

Jacklyn demonstrated leadership ability and a sense of responsibility in her position as a team supervisor and as an executive interviewer dealing with business professionals. A particularly difficult assignment required Jacklyn to interface with ophthalmic surgeons on a one-to-one basis. Her professionalism and communication skills earned her the praises of the surgeons as well as her supervisors. Her capabilities are always in evidence as are her continuing good humor and positive attitude.

It was a pleasure to have Jacklyn on our staff. She will be an asset to future employers both in her contribution to the workplace and in her relationship with her colleagues.

Sincerely,

Andrew Brand
Vice President

Figure 6.3

Jacklyn also had other letters of recommendation that verified the content of this letter. This consistent praise of Jacklyn's skills provided her with a powerful tool to differentiate herself from others. Make sure you build your own set of letters praising your skills so you will also benefit from this powerful tool! You can use them as an attachment to your resume and have others available for use in an interview.

Tip #20 – You must persuade the employer you are the best qualified person for the job.

Your resume has gotten you in the door for a job interview. Now it is time to "close the sale" by persuading the employer you're the best qualified person to fill the job and help the company achieve its goals. You do this by exhibiting a positive attitude, a desire for the job, and proving your skills match the job requirements.

Preparation for a specific job interview starts with research. You need to have an understanding of the employer's business and industry so you have a context in which to present your skills. Don't be someone who arrives for an interview knowing little about the company and its industry. This principle also applies if you're pursuing positions in nonprofit organizations, schools, healthcare, or government. You need to be able to demonstrate how your skills can help the organization meet its goals.

Good sources of information are the company's web-site, annual report, industry trade association websites, and internet search engines. Also most employers will list qualifications they desire in applicants for jobs they wish to fill. You should request this information so you can match your skills against these requirements.

Tip #21 – Use your positioning statement as a communication guide when engaged in an interview.

Your positioning statement provides a perfect communication guide for an interview, because it explains why you're qualified for the job. Use specific examples to demonstrate your skills and experience. Telling stories of how you applied your skills is more interesting and also provides the opportunity to show your communication skills and real work experience.

Listen carefully to the interviewer's comments and questions to ensure you understand what she or he is asking, and to ensure you respond in ways that effectively tell your story. Steer the conversation, but without forcing it, in a way that allows you to highlight how your skills and experience apply to the job you desire.

Also to perform well in a job interview, it is extremely important you understand the job interview strategies employers may use to assess you, and the types of questions you could be asked.

For example, they may ask questions about your past job responsibilities and experience, or ask you to provide examples that demonstrate your skills. You may be asked problem solving questions, or what you would do in hypothetical situations. They may deliberately create stressful situations to see how you react.

Information regarding interview strategies or questions can be easily obtained via an internet search using key words such as "interview strategies" or "interview questions". If you fail to perform the research and understand this information, you will most likely have a poor interview performance.

Lastly, employers want to hire employees who are hard working, highly motivated, responsible, dependable, goal directed, self-confident, able to perform under pressure, and capable of adapting to changing conditions. The more you can demonstrate these attributes, the greater the advantage you will have when competing for a job. Therefore, make sure you seize every opportunity to show you have these attributes in the stories you tell in your job interview. Also refer to your letters of recommendation to back up your claims.

Chapter 7

Find Job Opportunities

Begin Your Career

The steps and principles discussed in this chapter apply to finding a job with all organizations whether its a company, hospital, clinic, school, government agency or non-profit organization, The examples I've used refer to finding a job with a company, but they apply to all types of organizations.

The first step in your job search is to assemble a list of target companies you would like to explore. Use your college career center, library, and on-line sources to research companies to build your list.

Some very good on-line secondary sources for company and industry information are provided in Figure 7.0.

On-Line Company Research Sources
www.vault.com
www,forbes.com
www.inc.com/inc5000
www.pars.com   (The Pulblic Registers Annual Report Services
www.quintcareers.com/volunteering (Non profit career resources}
Individual company websites
Figure 7.0

Annual reports and company websites can also inform you about a company's growth and profit performance. Your goal should be to launch your career with a company that is performing well. This is important because good performing companies will provide opportunities for you to grow on the job.

If you have a geographic preference for where you want to live, be mindful that the number of opportunities available to you may vary depending on the area you've chosen. However, where you live will significantly impact your lifestyle, and therefore you should consider it carefully before starting your job search.

A variety of sources are available to help you search for jobs with the companies on your target list. They include:

College Career Center.
The career center organizes campus visits and career fairs for company recruiters to interview graduating students. Companies on your target list may be among them, or you may want to expand your list to include companies that will be visiting your campus.

The center offers other supplemental services to assist you in your job search. You should learn about the services of your school's career center upon enrollment in your college and use the center as a resource throughout your college years.

Direct Contact
Direct contact can be made with a company on your list. Many companies list jobs they want to fill on their website, and provide a procedure you can use to submit an application. Check target company websites for this application process.

Companies With Whom You've Interned.
Sometimes an internship leads to a job offer. The company knows you through your work as an intern and may wish to offer you a job after graduation. Because you've had the opportunity to learn what it is like to work for the company, you're in a great position to evaluate an offer. If a job is not available, or this company is not on your list, ask the people you've worked with to help you identify job opportunities with other companies on your target list.

Mentors
Your mentors may be able to help you identify job opportunities with companies on your target list, or help you start a networking effort to find people who can. Networking should play an ongoing role in your career.

Linkedin

Linkedin.com is a great networking tool you can use to build professional relationships that can lead to job referrals. It's also a good source to search for job opportunities..

Internet job search services.
Various job search websites offer services to find entry level job opportunities. A fee may be required to use the service.

The number of jobs available at a given point in time varies with the strength of the overall economy and the industry you've selected. If jobs are limited at the time you're entering your career, your search may take longer, and the competition for those jobs will be greater. However, skill development gives you an edge regardless of the strength of the job market.

Build Your Career

Building your career takes thought and action. It's important to be proactive rather than simply reactive to to events as they unfold. This principle is expressed in the following tip.

Tip #22 – Becoming aware and acting on advancement opportunities is essential to building your career.

Advancement of your career can be achieved with promotions within your current company or by accepting a position with another company.

Promotions are earned by those who stand out through excellent job performance that produces positive results for their employer. A great way for you to create opportunities to demonstrate your skills and increase your visibility within your company is to volunteer for team assignments. Working on teams is also a good way to learn more about your company's business, since team members are often assigned from multiple functional areas.

Recruiting a career mentor is another important way to help you build your career. The combination of excellent job performance and guidance from a career mentor is a very powerful way to build your career. This person can be someone in your company or industry who is willing to share his or her experience and advice to help you improve and move ahead. Many articles have been published about how to recruit a career mentor. You can find them on-line.

Building a network of professional friends is also an important and effective way to discover career opportunities and improve your industry knowledge and job skills. The purpose of this type of networking is to build a circle of professional friends whom you get to know well by helping each other. Sharing advice on work issues or working together in industry associations are great ways to build these friendships. Professional friendships take time and effort to build, but are personally very satisfying and provide support when you need it.

Another factor you will need to deal with in building your career is the rapid development of new technology.

Tip #23 – Make sure you understand the impact technology advances will have on your career, and be resilient to change.

Technology advances are occurring at an ever faster rate, and they can have a tremendous impact on your career. New technology changes the way things are done and requires you to develop new skills or be left behind. For example, the widespread use of the PC and software applications has created tremendous change in the workplace. This technology is second nature to you, but when it first emerged, people had to learn new skills and adapt to change. Technology driven change will be a big part of your future work life, and reinventing your skill set to adapt to the technology will be critical to your success.

Chapter 8

Assess Job Opportunities

Tip #24 – **Understand the key factors that affect your career growth.**

To properly assess job opportunities, it's important to understand your career advancement will be influenced by key factors that shape the environment in which you compete. These factors include:

- The state of the industry in which you work.
- Your company's success in achieving its goals.
- Your company's culture.
- The professional network you have built.

Your career advancement will also be influenced by the following factors that drive your job performance:

- The strength of your hard and soft skills.
- Amount of your work experience.
- Your skill development needs.

Figure 8.0 illustrates the interrelationship of these factors. Your career goals are represented by the circle at the center of the diagram. Your hard and soft skills, work experience, plus skill development needs are depicted in overlapping circles behind your career goals. *This illustrates the achievement of career goals is accomplished with a combination of continuously improving skills and work experience.*

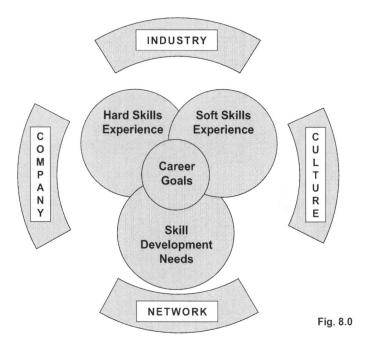

Fig. 8.0

Factors that shape the environment in which you compete are represented in the outer ring. For example, job opportunities will be more plentiful if you work in an <u>industry</u> that is growing rapidly, rather than an industry in decline. Likewise greater opportunity will exist if you work for a <u>company</u> that is growing and is able to compete successfully.

Your company's <u>culture</u> will also affect you in many ways. Company culture defines the personality and character of the company. It's a reflection of the company's core values, beliefs, employee behavior, work atmosphere, and management style. Cultures vary depending on the choices companies make with respect to issues like those listed below.

- The priority a company places on meeting customer needs.

- Emphasis on effective leadership and teamwork.

- Importance of innovation to the company's approach to its business.

- Level of commitment to employee development and empowerment.

- Reward for good job performance

- Degree of adaptability to changing conditions.

Your work environment will be determined by the culture of the company you join. For example, companies that place a high priority on meeting their customers' needs generally are more responsive to changing market conditions. Servicing the customer is the rallying theme management uses to motivate all company departments to work together as a team. As a result, all employees know the importance of their role in achieving customer satisfaction and understand market success is the result of teamwork.

Companies that are less focused on meeting their customers needs usually are slow to adjust to changing market conditions, and tend to exhibit less teamwork. The energy and satisfaction that comes from meeting company goals through teamwork is usually missing in these types of companies.

As you can see, your work experience would be very different in the two types of companies described above. Likewise, a company that values employee training and empowers employees to make decisions will be different from one that provides little training and is very authoritarian. Or a company that rewards its employees based on good job performance will provide more opportunity than one that bases rewards on favoritism. Finding a company whose culture is a good fit for you is very important to achieving the happiness and success you seek in your work.

The last element of the outer ring of Figure 8.0 is a network of mentors and professional friends. Creating such a network will increase the number of opportunities available to you by growing your skills and by increasing your awareness of chances for advancement within your company and industry.

Evaluate Job Offers

The model illustrated in Figure 8.0 is a very useful aid for evaluating a job offer, since it focuses on the most important factors affecting your career advancement. For example, when you launch your career and are evaluating job offers, you should carefully assess the company and its culture. Join a company that has good sales and profit performance and a culture that will give you the opportunity to perform well and enhance your skills with job experience. Look for a culture that values employee development, offers training, and provides advancement opportunities based on good job performance. Your goal is to get off to a good start and build a solid base of experience.

Obtain the information you need to make this assessment from the pre-interview company research you do and your job interview. Although it takes working in a company for awhile to really know its culture, you can get a reasonable feel for it by asking the right questions.

For example, following are some questions you could ask when given an opportunity in your interview.

- What qualities do your most successful employees possess?

- What skills are most important to be able to perform well in this job?

- What opportunities are there for additional training and education ?

- What career paths have been established for employees in this position?

- Could you please describe the management style of the company?

- What do you like about working for the company?

Listen carefully to the answers to develop a feel for the culture. You'll spend a lot of time on the job, so it's important the culture is a good fit for you.

As your career develops, you may be presented with opportunities to work in new companies or a different industry. Evaluating those opportunities will be most effective by considering the interrelationships illustrated in Figure 8.0.

If the opportunity is a job in a different company, the first question to ask yourself is: Will the new job help me achieve my career goals? A good tool to use for making this evaluation is to rate the job opportunity on a list of criteria that relate to your career goals.

For example, you might list things like the salary being offered, opportunity for advancement, how interesting and challenging the job will be, the independence you will be given to act in the job, your ability to impact results, and the risk you take in accepting the job.

Assign a rating of 1 to 5 (with 5 being best) for each criteria. The ratings will help you visualize how the job opportunity measures up to your personal criteria. It is especially helpful if you are evaluating multiple job offers. The checklist below illustrates this technique.

CRITERIA	JOB 1	JOB 2
Salary	4	5
Opportunity For Advancement	5	3
Interesting / Challenging Job	4	4
Independence To Act	3	2
My Impact On Results	4	2
Risk	3	2

Figure 8.1

The next questions you should ask are do I have the hard and soft skills to be successful? What skills do I need to improve or acquire? Is the company and its culture right for me? What advice should I seek from my network?

If a change in industry is involved, your evaluation should include an analysis of the industry's characteristics and growth prospects, and how your skills and past experience relate and prepare you to be successful.

Tip #25 – To evaluate a job opportunity at any stage of your career, ask yourself three questions:

- Will this job help me achieve my career goals?

- Do I have the skills and experience required to be successful in this job?

- Will my work environment support the achievement of my career goals?

Chapter 9

<u>Conclusion</u>

My goal is to help you achieve happiness and success in your work life. I invited you on a journey to learn how to find work that is interesting and rewarding, and to build skill advantages that will help you get the job you want.

The journey started with a process to select an interesting occupation that is a match for your talents. It continued with identifying and developing skills required to succeed. The last leg of the journey explored ways to market yourself and to find and assess job opportunities. My 25 tips provide a roadmap that charts a journey from discovery of career interests to success in the work world.

Currently most students don't undertake the skill building journey I've described in this book. Others who read this book will not have the discipline to follow through. The ball is now in your hands. Will you run with it to find work you love, and create skill advantages that will help you win the job you want? If you do, you will be miles ahead of your competition.

Go for it!

APPENDIX

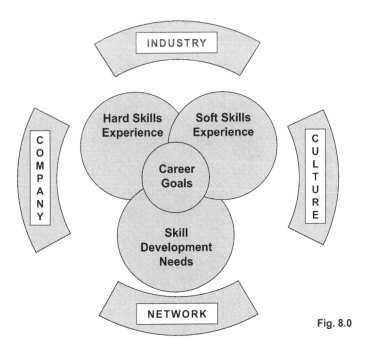

Fig. 8.0

Your career advancement will be influenced by key factors that drive your job performance. These factors include:

- The strength of your hard and soft skills.
- Amount of your work experience.
- Your skill development needs.

Figure 8.0 illustrates the interrelationship of these factors. Your career goals are represented by the circle at the center of the diagram. Your hard and soft skills, work experience, plus skill development needs are depicted in overlapping circles behind your career goals. This illustrates the achievement of career goals is accomplished with a combination of continuously improving skills and work experience.

Your career advancement will also be influenced by key factors that shape the environment in which you compete. These factors include:

- The state of the industry in which you work.
- Your company's success in achieving its goals.
- Your company's culture.
- The professional network you have built.

It is critical to your success that these factors are supportive of your career goals.

The model illustrated in Figure 8.0 is also a very useful tool to help you evaluate new job opportunities.

Tip Sheet

Your ability to compete is the single most important factor in determining the success you will have in your work life.

You have the power to make choices now that will greatly improve your ability to succeed and gain what you want in the future.

Tip # 1 – The best time for you to start exploring occupations is when you enter high school.

Tip # 2 – Learning to compete in the workplace requires practice, just as learning any new skill requires practice.

Tip # 3 – A good appearance is important, and like it or not, people form opinions of you based on appearance and first impressions.

Tip # 4 – Being prepared to make the most of a meeting is an important skill you will need in the workplace.

Tip # 5 – A mentor relationship is extremely valuable. He or she will share his or her experience and advice, thus giving you a tremendous advantage in developing your career.

Tip # 6 – The more highly you develop skills that are important to employers, the more successful you will become.

Tip # 7 – Highly developed soft skills play a big role in creating competitive advantage.

Tip # 8 – The fact that employers desire the ideal in an employee creates a great opportunity for those willing to practice positive personal attributes. By combining these attributes and other soft skills with hard skill excellence, you'll be highly valuable to employers and experience great success.

Tip # 9 – To build skill advantages, you need to know where you want to go with your career.

Tip # 10 – Participation in extra curricular activities and part-time jobs provides great opportunities to learn and practice soft skills.

Tip # 11 – The extra effort it takes to work on soft skills in extra curricular activities and part-time jobs is small, but the benefits are huge!

Tip # 12 – Keep a record of how you used soft skills in your activities and jobs.

Tip # 13 – Request letters of recommendation from supervisors in all the jobs you hold.

Tip # 14 – The use of alumni mentors and working in internships is an absolute necessity to gain the most from your college education.

Tip # 15 – Seeking advice from a career mentor is the most effective way to improve your skills and build your career.

Tip # 16 – You should think of yourself as a product. Create a positioning that is based on your skill advantages.

Tip # 17 – Understand the employer's hiring perspective.

Tip # 18 – Resumes that quickly communicate; "I'm qualified – I have the skills to do the job!", trigger interviews.

Tip # 19 – Show proof of your skills on your resume.

Tip # 20 – You must persuade the employer you are the best qualified for the job.

Tip # 21 – Use your positioning statement as a communication guide when engaged in an interview.

Tip # 22 – Becoming aware and acting on advancement opportunities is essential to building your career.

Tip # 23 – Make sure you understand the impact technology advances will have on your career, and be resilient to change.

Tip # 24 – Understand the key factors that affect your career growth.

Tip # 25 – To evaluate a job opportunity at any stage of your career, ask yourself two questions:

- Do I have the skills and experience required to be successful in this job?

- Will my work environment support the achievement of my career goals?

Made in the USA
Coppell, TX
16 January 2020

14583973R10046